Impressions
&
Expressions

An Anthology of Poems

Dominic Arivarasu Mathias

BookLeaf Publishing

India | USA | UK

Presentation by *BookLeaf Publishing*

Web: www.bookleafpub.com

E-mail: info@bookleafpub.com

ISBN: 9789360944544

First edition 2024

ACKNOWLEDGEMENT

I am greatly indebted to my better half, Maria Mathalan and my children, Merin Glinta and Jovita, for being my first and best critics. In spite of the late hours, they always took the time to review my writings and suggest improvements. They mirror all my readers. The final shape of every poem owes much to all the three.

Thank you Glinta and Andrew for the beautifully designed meaningful cover.

Sincere thanks to my elder twin Fr Arularasu Mathias from the Diocese of Corpus Christi, TX, for being the motivating factor in all my endeavours.

Thank you BookLeaf Publishing team for making this book a reality.

PREFACE

Although Plato rated philosophy to be higher than poetry, what is a poem devoid of some sort of philosophizing? Undoubtedly, every poet is a philosopher!

The poems in this anthology were mostly written over a period of time. It includes some poems on the most common themes of love and nature, besides some reflective and narrative poems. The arrangement of poems is not thematic, in the sense that they do not adhere to a pre-planned theme. But they are the result of the impressions of people and events on me. Conspicuous by their absence are too many literary devices such as figures of speech, meter and rhyme. This frugality is intended to keep the reader glued to the narrative without indulging in divergent distractions.

My message to the budding poet is that you need not wait for an outpouring of inspiration from Plato's World of Ideas to start writing. Any mundane experience or visual can be the subject matter for a poem. Keep your mind plain like a tabula rasa, a blank slate, and let impressions stick on it. You can design a poem or a narrative out of it.

Happy reading.

Table of Contents

Miss You Nights

Twelve years of hugs and caresses…
Suddenly you have disappeared!
I crave for your touch, unsatiated, inconsolate

Sometimes I see you pass by,
Hear your voice linger like cool mist.
But you vanish as fast as you appear
Before I could relish reminiscences of
yesteryears

Someone else owns me now.
He has become a part of my life
And I his.
He's heavy on me, unlike you.
Adjusting is hard you know

He visits me in the wee hours, a busy man,
Like you used to during the lockdown days.
It is a second lockdown for me now
But I am glad of his truncated hours

I yearn for your tresses, though scanty, on me
Caressing me, enveloping me,
Their aroma engulfing and
Lingering through the day.

Thinking of it, I tremble

Return please, return to me
Your every twist and turn was sheer ecstasy.

How I wish to be reborn as a human being
So that I may reciprocate your comforting touch,
Hugging you in return!

Because only a human being can do it
Not a pillow like me on your bed

Eternity

You thrust my heart with a dart
Whenever I behold you
My mind empties on you.
Intact when thou art within
And mindless when without

Perched on a camel's hind
Yearn I for a ride
With you by my side
Clasping from behind
Chugging past wayward bushes
Your bosom embracing my back

Camel lazing on sand dunes
Ebbing and surging clack clack
Massaging to soothing tunes
On the undulation all around

Oh eternity, this is eternity!
This is heaven
I need no heaven
Till the end of eternity
Save you beside me.

Freeze the moment please
In a tight embrace

Leave Me as I AM

Poses to be veritably humble
Flaunts humility on his sleeves
Professes it to all and sundry
Listing out, simultaneously, all his achievements

Says he, "Who wants a name?
Ephemeral, it is.
Who wants fame?
It is elusive

Of course, I have done 1001 things
Received accolades from fora galore
Still enabling others, elevating them

Mind you, you are privy to this
Because, I reiterate, I need no name or fame

I am empowered
Now I'll take on the world,
Devoid of value system and morality.
I am on a mission of transformation

Why don't they learn from me?
See how selfless I am!
Harmless but straightforward.
Hate me for my forthrightness
But, leave you, I won't
Till your cocoon cracks
And I see a new you –
Not just you but everybody:
The whole world.

I shall conspire with the universe
And rest not till your back breaks
And our tunes match

For humble am I.
Do I trumpet my strengths
Like my neighbour?
Am I devious like her?"

His blabbering and blathering hound me
Till I find my heels
And flee with no backward glance

Leave me, I murmur,

I am what I am
I don't want no change in me
Don't want to be your victim
Love me as I am or leave me as I am

'Brother'

Feather-touch it was
Seemingly innocuous, unthreatening
A fleeting caress
In a fleeting moment.

In her every glance there was corroboration
Of intimacy, of intrigue.
Was it mere illusion?

Days and nights were fleeing
Like a lengthening shadow in the fading light.

An inscrutable elation this morning
And bliss seems within reach.

Ecstasy intoxicates me.

'Brother,' she beckons me.

Crashes this word on my lap
Like the hammer of Thor
Tearing up my entrails
Smashing them to smithereens

That Elusive Dream

'Rouse the writer in you
The world is your canvas
Your masterpiece beckons you.'

Euphonic the clarion call.
Mesmerizes the monumental optimist
Nursing a dormant Shakespearean muse

'Attend my FREE Masterclass
Soon a published author you will be
Earning income even post demise.'

Testimonies lure ingenuous aspirants.
Failed attempts and agonies
Urging 'em with a fragile resolve:
'Publish my book I will,
Not in 90 or 30 but in 10 days!'

The marketing maverick harangues:
'Join my mission
To catapult you to the skies.

My package is worth millions
But pay a paltry XXX sum.
Pittance it is, considering its worth and value.
Pay up in 15 minutes
Life-long support, my guarantee.
Don't regret after fifteen minutes.'

The gullible guy empties his kitty
Half-hoping a Cinderella to do his bidding
Naive eyes fail the fine print of
The exacting conditions to publish in a fortnight.

Finds no time for creativity
An hour-a-day is beyond reach.

A fortnight flies
A month meanders
The ambitious tome remains elusive.

Heaves a sigh when months slide stealthily:
'Thank heavens I didn't part with millions
But a few thousand bucks!'

Maybe writing is not in my blood.
Maybe I will begin after retirement.

*[**Disclaimer: This poem is meant for light
entertainment. Its intention is NOT to belittle the
work of any mentor and/or publisher.]*

Mommy Versus Wifey

Mom would say: Boys, kitchen isn't your place
Stay clear of it.
Now my wife says: Kitchen isn't my private
space
Why am I alone in it?

Mom dines after dad, alone
Wife says: Who will eat alone?
Mom says: Marriages are made in heaven
Wife says: To hell with you if me you ignore

Mommy: My bank balance? Ask my hubby
Wifey: My money is mine, I earned it buddy
Mommy: I birthed you and made you a man
Wifey: You are mine forever, Kiddoo

My mom was my first love

My wife was also my first love!
Mom seems old-fashioned
Wife is upbeat and upmarket

Sandwiched between Scylla and Charybdis
The devil and the deep sea
(*God forbid, any of them reads this!*)
Choice and reason elude me
Making me a lousy mousey

Sunset

Sinking steadily behind waters yonder
As millions cheer the winterly spectacle
Applauding himself contentedly
The sun god bids goodbye to the globe

A misty veil mocks viewers
Silhouetting the Helios.
The frenzied clicks of zillion shutters
Outnumber celebrated celebrities'

Shadows overshadow good with bad
Time for bats and badgers
Celebratory parties to toast the day gone by
Relationships eternalized by moony mates

Crowning glory of the dying day,

The moon tiptoes from nowhere
Picking up pieces left by her pal
As Romeos whisper sweet nothings to Juliets.

Time the Revealer

With a ready wit on his lips
He seemed self-effacing, down to earth.
What a pleasant personality, they admired
Jolly good fella really.

Revealing his fangs by and by
Nasty knave he turned out to be
With a vanishing grin and hardened chin
Grinding teeth and fiery eyes

Presumptuous, petulant and petty
He unfriended friend and foe
Distancing from one and all
En route to his purgatory

Humour and wit but the façade
To disguise unaccepted identity
Jealous of the gayer multitude
Powerless to match them

'Unfit for his position,' now they snarl

'Demote him,' they murmur
'Dispatch him,' rise the chorus

Unaware of his insecurity
The demons he was fighting
Heart brimming with bitterness and angst.

Alas! Time reveals all
But does it really heal?

An Infant's First Tryst with the Ocean

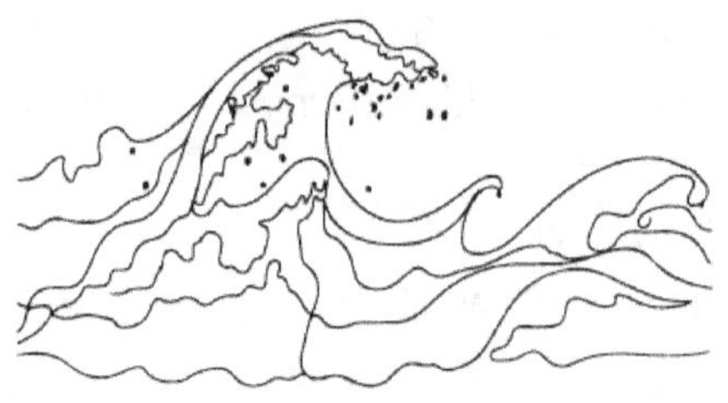

Beneath a cloudless canopy blue
Sprawls an endless azure sheet
Parted by pearly grainy strips

Call it sea or ocean or waters.
Cold when dad dips my leg
Bubbles befriending feeble feet
Cooling caresses tickling my soles.

Flees like a truant before I grasp,
Wandering eyes wondering in awe.
Right on cue, outward she races
Stronger and larger and faster

Mum drops my feet this time
Through the foam touching the sand.
Mischievous foams dart around
Smearing little grains on little legs.

Giggling, we play hide and seek
Till she turns yellow grey and gold,
Residue of the waning sun.

The ocean becomes dark and cold
Transmitting me to mother's womb
Whispering into my ears:
'We are one babe:
You the ocean, I the wave.'

Fatherhood – First Day

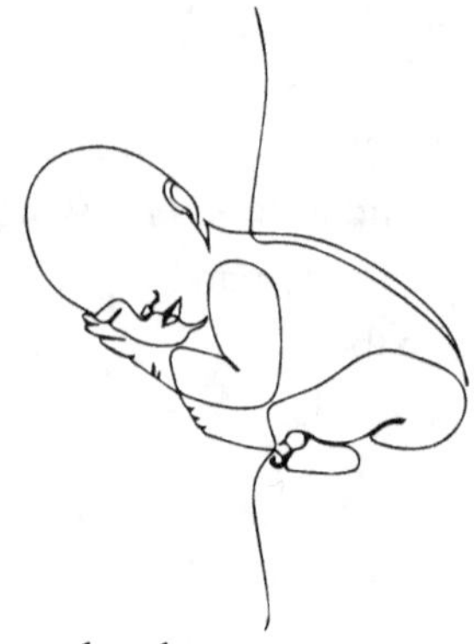

A sculptor labours hard
Chipping away the superfluous,
Extracting the figure,
Revealing the masterpiece

A potter spins his wheel
Shaping the pot with adept hands
Stamping designs with dexterous fingers.

Monumental miracle indeed
To hold you in my arms
Minutes after your birth

Oh, those amazing features!
Rounded nostrils, hair dark and dense, unseeing
eyes
Overgrown nails on frail fingers.

The potter and sculptor
Shape the exterior
But you surpass the peripheral

Full and complete you are,
With bones and ligaments and flesh
Brain and lungs and muscle
All that is needed for a lifetime!

No wonder
A potter needs hours
A sculptor shapes in a week
While your Creator bears you nine months
Within the warm womb of your mother

If I could fly…

If I could fly…
Will I flee from ungrateful Homo sapiens?
Will I flee from conceited humans?
Flee from egotistical brats?
From unthinking beasts?

Or from the one who rejected my overtures?
Or the ones who are at my heels in close
pursuit?
Or the one who's awaiting a faux pax to betray
me?
Or from the one who's ever ready to belittle me?

No. None of these!

I want to fly away from the one who knows
himself

I want to fly away from the one who's ever
suspicious
I want to fly away from the one who reads my
thoughts
I want to fly away from the one who apprehends
my motives

Who's this villain?
Who is this devil?
What if that devil is but.... Me?

Life - a Seesaw

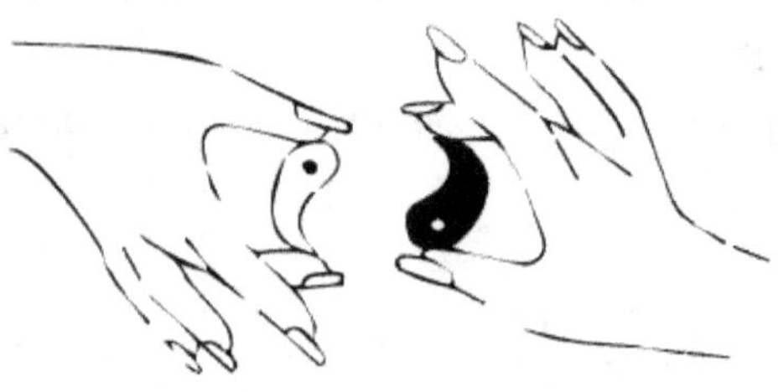

Life.
A seesaw they say.
I see it now and saw it then.

Every present is a past
Viewed in a fleeting second
Like a film strip, pixelated.

Connections are darned twixt micro-images
Wrenching meaning out of them
Like a palmist deciphering the crease on your
palms.

Coz I Am Only a Woman

Expectation precedes disappointment
But friendship necessitates expectations
And love encompasses expectations

What about marriage?
Doesn't it entail expectations?
Is fidelity too much of an expectation?
Should arranged marriages belie expectations?

Every man has a history.
Can't a girl too have a history?
Oh man, you come with your baggage.
What about me?

How much do you know me
My family, my struggles

My anxiety, my rejection
My reticence caused by self-doubt?

How can I forget him who lifted me up
First with a smile
Then with words
Sharing his food packet -
Most of all
Listening to me!
He made me what I am
Made me look up and smile with confidence
How can I relinquish him!

You could not forget your flame
But I had to forgo my man!

For me you were my world
But I was just your moon, a satellite.

Your escapades in the moonlight
Broke my heart.
But never did I retaliate or reciprocate
Not because I didn't love him

But because I am I, a woman
And you are you, a man.

Drawing Straight with Crooked Sticks

Heated, water boils
Beaten, metal softens
Action – Reaction
Cause – Effect

Goodness is rewarded, they say
But good people suffer.
Evil will self-destruct, they say
But evil destroys others.
Action – Adverse Reaction
Cause and effect? No way

Suspect your beloved.
She is hurt, and you are hurt.
Misjudge your mates
They grieve, and you too.
Cause and effect? No way

Infidelity is but presumed.

Lucky portent a child becomes
If promotion follows birth.
Harbinger of bad omen
In case of tragedy.
Post hoc, ergo propter hoc
(After this, therefore, on account of this.)
Cause and effect? No way

Two and two maybe four on earth.
In the unfathomable expanse of outer space
It could be 22, 222, 202 or something else!
Mysterious, the ways of the cosmos
Cause and effect, mere illusions.
Hence the saying:
God draws straight with crooked sticks.

Love, not Lust

Your reticence spoke volumes
Your silence was loud
You understood my loneliness
My need for companionship

Pig iron I was in a furnace
For you a diamond in a coal heap

Your distance was a lodestone
Prying eyes, a double-edged sword

My cravings you resisted
For you knew I couldn't be yours
Nor you mine

When you surrendered
Love it was, not lust

I abstained, helpless
'Coz love it was, not lust

You eased into my life gradually
I exited from yours all at once
Did you long for me? Ever?

No. Don't answer me
Don't misunderstand me
For it was love, not lust.

Rich versus Poor

Mumbai, a great leveler thou art
Making the rich and the poor rub shoulders
In trains, buses, and auto rickshaws.

While patiently queuing under the blistering sun
at the Gateway
To purchase tickets for a joyride into the sea
Who is rich and who is poor?

When sitting impatiently for my name to be
called
At a doctor's clinic or hospital
Who is rich and who is poor?

While relaxing in a multiplex
And watching my favourite movie
Who is rich and who is poor?

But
When he hires a cab from Nariman Point to
CSMT
Instead of waiting for carpooling,
I know who is affluent and who isn't

When he travels by first class
While my life gets squeezed out in the second
I know who can afford and who cannot

When he buys a single malt
While I look for the cheap-and-best IMFL
I know who is who

The pomfret and Bombay duck on Wednesdays
and Fridays
And the type of meat on their plates on Sundays
Reveal who is rich and who is not

But
When I hear the chant 'Ram Naam Satya Hai'
While being carried away on the last journey
It doesn't matter who is rich and who is poor

The Girl in a Blue Cardigan

Armed with a degree in Philosophy
And training in pedagogy
Stormed I into the ninth class
To teach Moral Science:
'Twas the first class of my career.

The topic was Free Will.
Does man have a free will?
If everything is God's creation
Evil must also be His handiwork.
Whither man's free will?

If only good can come out of good,
How can a good God create evil?
Is God then an admixture of good and evil?
The questions seemed ominous
And arguments valid

Using all my knowledge
And expertise in Theodicy,
Ethics and Anthropology
My views I expounded
To a silent audience
A group of first-generation learners

Using high-sounding terminology
And references to Nietzsche
Kierkegaard and Sartre
I talked about weltanschauung
And sundry concepts,
Eager to exhibit my erudition,
Knowing that the first impression is a lasting
one.

When the bell rang
Patting my back on a job well done
In that remote village in Meghalaya
I bowed out of the room
With a smile on my lips
Contented and complacent.

Was gladdened by a visit at lunch
Of a plump and portly girl
To my chamber, definitely to appreciate:
"How did you like my class?
Spotted you smiling throughout."

With a twinkle on her face
Hiding a grin with her right hand
Holding her snug blue cardigan with her left
Said she, "Sir, I came here to tell you…
On behalf of the whole class…
That we understood not a word of what you
taught!"

Stunned I was. Speechless. Shattered
All my confidence and contentment
Dashed to the ground.

The girl in the blue cardigan
Taught me to understand my students
Before venturing into exposition:
Alas, communication becomes futile
Unless comprehended!

That girl in the blue cardigan
Taught me on the first day of my career
How to teach, transforming me
Into a life-long learner-by-profession
Which I am today.

Reward, a Demotivator?

'You will be rewarded.'
Was it a compliment or condescension?
Or dismissal as a subordinate?

Flabbergasted I was.
Intrigued

Boy, it was meant to motivate!
That sure was her motive:
Reward to motivate
Dangle carrot for favour.

Bribe it is for sure
When promised in advance

Your salary, your reward?
'Nyet'
'Tis compensation for service,
Deserved as per covenant.
Salary ain't a gift

Coz it's earned

Reward being gratis
Is whimsical, mostly.

Working for a reward
You enslave yourself
And the donor enslaves you too:
You dance to their tunes

While being assured of a reward
Was I being beguiled for a favour?

My reward is my work:
My work is my reward
Contentment with my job

Not your approbation
Not aught external.
Welcome, though they are

Promise me not a reward.
Never.
Keep the goodies for yourself
May your reward adorn your bosom
And swell your ego
Not me nor mine.

Vintage Years

'Life may be a maleficent sadist.
But I am her elder sister,' she rants.

Her face tells a different story, though:
Drooping eyes, raised eyebrows
Saggy cheeks and convex lips

Bricks and bamboos have been her lot,
None of those candies and cookies.

'Such a bigoted brute you are!
Your reward to a thirty minuter
Equals mine, a full day labourer.
I have my right; pay me my dues.'

'You signed up for your lot,' quoth he.
'I am the Master
Don't you resent my kindness.'

'To hell with your contract
Shed your arrogant bounty:
I toiled more; I deserve more.'

'You're past your prime, my lady,' jeer her
peers.
'Shed your conceit, shelve your greed.
'Tis time you enjoyed your vintage years.

Get ready for a toothless age and unwalking legs
When you'll dance to others' tunes,
A doll in a kid's hands

Drink your life to its dregs today.
Live your life when it is yours
It's the final quarter of your life.'

Poor soul!
Oblivious of bitching behind her back
She struts her superior self
Like a peacock in its vintage years.

Dad's Wish

Happy to see you settled, son
What do you want from me when I am gone?

Nothing dad
Give me but the Holy Book that you use
And the Dictionary on your shelf.
Both are timeless.

Dad bade goodbye to the world
Leaving all to his daughters
All but the house to his lone son
And of course the Holy Book and the dictionary.

A grandfather now, with pride in heart
He points at the Holy Book and the dictionary
'These are my most prized possessions.'

'But they are old grandpa,' says the grandkid,
'Outdated they are!

There are better versions and more modern.'

'But it's my father's legacy my love
Preserve them for posterity.'

With a lowered gaze GenZ stands before his
dad:
'Great grandpa is gone, and grandpa is aged
What if we throw this junk away dad?
Will his soul lose its solace?
Hasn't he gone to heaven yet?
Or still waiting to check on his books?
Maybe it was close to grandpa and his dad
Not to me. I don't want them.
Please, dad.'

'Our ancestors were pure at heart
Heaven was theirs on demise.
Sentiment is a blinder, son.
The books are yours to discard.'

'Love you Dad.'

The Surrender

Blessed among women, I thought
Don Juan of my office
Fall in love? Never, I bragged

Her first day in office
Her amiable arrogance intrigued me
Tame her I will, I averred
A game of cat and mouse I will play
Blowing fire and ice.

Oblivious of my intentions she ignored me
'Twas not vanity but naïveté
And innocence, I realized.

Beyond approach she became
Blowing fire and ice
Playing a game of cat and mouse

Her giggles and rustic wit were pure magic
Eventually it was I who surrendered
Not the amorous sweet li'l rustic.

www.ingramcontent.com/pod-product-compliance
Lightning Source LLC
LaVergne TN
LVHW021257200726
843509LV00012B/1704